WHOOO...
WHOOO...

Rourke
Publishing LLC
Vero Beach, Florida 32964

HERE COME THE TRAINS

Molly Carroll
Jeanne Sturm

www.rourkepublishing.com

PHOTO CREDITS: Title page: © Jonathan Larsen; page 3: © Jason Alan; page 4: © Chris Kruger; page 5: © Sherwin Mcgehee; page 6: © Chris Kruger; page 7: © Terraxplorer; pages 8-9: © Hugo de Wolf; pages 10-11: © Robert Simon; pages 12-13: © Bobo11 (wikipedia.com); pages 14-15: © Niknikon; pages 16-17: © Don Wilkie; pages 18-19: © Scott Griessel; pages 20-21: © Alex Slobodkin

Editor: Kelli Hicks

Cover design by: Nicola Stratford: bdpublishing.com

Interior design by: Renee Brady

Library of Congress Cataloging-in-Publication Data

Carroll, Molly.
  Whooo, whooo ... here come the trains / Molly Carroll, Jeanne Sturm.
    p. cm. -- (My first discovery library)
  Includes bibliographical references and index.
  ISBN 978-1-60472-528-5
  1. Railroad trains--Juvenile literature. I. Sturm, Jeanne. II. Title.
  TF148.C295 2009
  625.1--dc22
                              2008025166

Printed in the USA

CG/CG

Rourke Publishing

www.rourkepublishing.com – rourke@rourkepublishing.com
Post Office Box 3328, Vero Beach, FL 32964

Have you ever seen a train zooming down the railroad tracks?

Full Speed Ahead!

Trains travel when it's dark.

People sleep, and
the train moves on.

Trains travel when it's light.

6

Dining cars serve food, and the train moves on.

High-speed trains go very fast.

Double-decker trains
carry people from
city to city.

Freight trains carry many things.

Freight cars carry coal.

15

Tanker cars carry oil.

17

Closed-in cars keep freight safe.

All aboard, and then
Full Speed Ahead!

Glossary

coal (KOHL): Coal is a hard, black mineral found underground. Coal is used as a fuel.

dining cars (DINE-ing KARZ): Dining cars are railroad cars that serve meals. Eating in a dining car is like eating in a restaurant, except you're on the move. On some double-decker trains, food is prepared on the lower level and diners eat on the upper level.

freight (FRAYT): Freight is cargo that is carried from place to place. Freight can be carried by ships, planes, trains, and trucks.

tanker (TANG-kur): Tanker cars, or tank cars, carry liquids such as oil and chemicals. If a train carrying dangerous chemicals in tanker cars crashes, people who live and work near the crash site may have to leave.

Index

Further Reading

Crowther, Robert. *Trains: A Pop-up Railroad Book*. Candlewick Press, 2006.

Sobel, June. *The Goodnight Train*. Harcourt, 2006.

Simon, Seymour. *Seymour Simon's Book of Trains*. HarperCollins Publishers, 2004.

Websites

http://www.trainwreckcentral2.com/kidsfun.html

http://home.howstuffworks.com/paper-trains.htm

About the Authors

Molly Carroll has been reading children's books since she was a baby. She loves reading them just as much today.

Jeanne Sturm and her family live in Florida, along with a very active dog, two friendly rabbits, and many colorful fish.